AHSHIÁ:TON
YOU SHOULD WRITE IT

Jules Delorme

BookLand
press

Published by
BookLand Press Inc.
15 Allstate Parkway, Suite 600
Markham, Ontario L3R 5B4
www.booklandpress.com

Front cover image by Jennifer Deschamps

Printed in Canada

Library and Archives Canada Cataloguing in Publication

Title: Ahshiá:ton: you should write it / Jules Delorme.
Names: Delorme, Jules, author.
Description: Series statement: Modern Indigenous voices
Identifiers: Canadiana (print) 20230182720 | Canadiana (ebook)
2023018278X | ISBN 9781772312102 (softcover) |
ISBN 9781772312119 (EPUB)
Subjects: LCGFT: Short stories.
Classification: LCC PS8607.E487565 A91 2023 | DDC C813/.6—dc23

We acknowledge the support of the Government of Canada through the Canada Book Fund and the support of the Ontario Arts Council, an agency of the Government of Ontario. We also acknowledge the support of the Canada Council for the Arts.

AHSHIÁ:TON
YOU SHOULD WRITE IT

Table of Contents

SITTIN WITH BACON PETE

-you ain't gonna make it till morning.

-why not. bacon pete said.

bug looked at bacon pete. wondered how he couldn't know.

-cuz. bug said -you been gutshot. you ain't gonna outlive that. bein gutshot.

-i got snakebit once. pete said -everybody said I was gonna die then but I didn't die.

-this is different.

-how. how exactly.

-i dunno pete. but them whitemen put a big size bullet in you.

pete tried to make himself comfortable. couldn't get it done.

-they put a big hole in you. a big ugly ole hole. bug said.

- everythin's comin out of you.

you ain't gonna live. not till mornin even.

-i might. pete didn't let go of a thing too easy.

-no. pete. bug said -you're gonna die.

pete thought about arguing some more. decided against it. bug wasn't exactly the fastest catfish in the creek. and he was all the way indian. all the way full blood indians were a whole different thing altogether. they believed crazy things even when it didn't make no sense to believe things. beside which pete's gut had a hole that was like a burning fire inside him and he couldn't get comfortable underneath that tree.

-it hurts. pete said.

-yeah. bug said -i guess it would.

bug knew a little bit about being shot. bug's father put a bullet through bug's shoulder once. he had been aiming for bug's heart but he was drunk and picked the wrong side and beside all that bug's father never could shoot for nothing, so he hit bug in the shoulder.

it still hurt sometime.

he guessed pete was feeling a whole lot worse.

-i wish i could keep you livin, pete. bug told pete -or make you not hurt till you die.

pete decided to just lie down in the grass for a little bit.

-i know. he said -i know you would. you're a good friend bug. i know you'd help me if you could.

they just waited for awhile. bug standing there and bacon pete lying in the grass. the sky was filled up with all kinds of stars.

-if i asked you to. bacon pete said -would you hunt down those whitemen and kill them.

bug thought about that. -probably. he said -probably i'd try to figure a way to do it so i don't go to jail but i'd probly go to jail anyways.

-probly get lynched. pete said -or stuck in the electric chair.

-that real.

-i dunno. pete said -i ain't gonna die anyways.

bug just stood there. pete could dig in with a thing some-
times. no point arguing about it. he looked down at the
hole in pete's stomach. even with pete's hand covering it,
it was a mighty big hole. that whiteman had just pointed
his fancy shiny rifle at poor pete and pulled the trigger.
sounded like thunder. then they all just rode away.
now bacon pete was going to die on account of not
knowing when to stay quiet.
there was nothing bug could do about it. fifteen miles
at least till the nearest for sure people. pete wasn't so
big but bug wasn't no louis cyr either. no way bug could
carry him across fifteen miles of wet bush. rain all week.
trails were nothing but mud and mush. he'd fall down
and drop pete for sure. no point in causing pete all that
pain when he wasn't even going to make it. bug thought
for awhile about maybe making a raft but by the time he
got that done pete'd already be dead and besides the
river was looking some kind of mean from the rain.
all bug could do was stand there and watch.
wait.
pete moved around a little on the grass. tried to find a
dry spot. whatever might be dry got all wet with his
blood but he tried it anyways. nothing else to do. try to
find a dry spot and maybe look up at the all those stars.
the tree.

-i hate this goddamn tree. bacon pete said.

bug looked at it.

-it's just a tree. he said.

-yeah i know it but i hate the darn thing anyways. pete looked at the tree for a while. hating it. -it's ugly. old and ugly. what kind of tree is that anyways.

-i don't know. maple maybe.

-that ain't maple. it ain't no maple tree. look at them leaves. it ain't no maple tree.

-then i guess i dunno what it is.

-indians are supposed to know that kind of thing. specially all the way indians.

bug shrugged. -it's just a tree pete. he said.

pete stared up at it with one eye. then the other. -i hate it. i hate that fuckin tree. pete said.

-you shouldn'ta argued with those whitemen. bug said.

-they were on rez land. pete said back.

-they had guns.

pete stared up at the stars. tried to remember if they were all in the right place.

-they wouldn'ta shot you if you hadda just shut up for awhile. bug said.

-i used to know where all the stars were supposed to be. bacon pete said

-no. you never.

-i did. my ole man showed me. i... um. i could tell where i was by the stars.

-no. you were always lost pete. long as i can remember you were gettin lost.

-my ole man was all the way indian. he... my ole man he knew things.'

-no. he was just a drunk like mine.

-he knew... uh. things.

bug walked over to the tree. looked at the leaves for a while.

-damn. pete said -feels like I gotta take the nastiest crap.

bug looked at bacon pete. sniffed the air.

-pretty sure you already took one pete. he said.

-no. 1 never.

-yeah i think you did. i can smell shit.

-i never crapped my pants in my my whole life.

-yeah but i think you just did.

pete went quiet. tried to smell it. all he could smell was burnt up copper and wet grass. animals smelled like burnt pennies sometimes when they got shot. he felt like he was looking at bug through some kind of candy wrapper wax paper or something. but he didn't smell shit. he guessed he'd smell it if he crapped himself. pete tried to sit up. so he could look down and see. but his head wouldn't move right. wouldn't do what he told it. it didn't feel connected to his body the way it was supposed to be.

-when you were a baby. bug said.

-what. pete said.

-i bet when you were a little baby you must've messed yourself so this is probly not the first time you ever did it.

-i don't know. pete said -but i bet... i bet i wasn't wearin pants then. what i said was that i never crapped my pants before... my... i said pants.

bug went quiet. he didn't have an answer for that. pete was stubborn when he was trying to make a point. that's how that bullet ended up inside him.

pete gave up trying to move around. he just lied there on the wet grass looking up.

-i bet they was yanks. pete said.

bug didn't answer. he just looked up at the leaves on the tree.

-they looked like yanks to me. pete said -brand new guns and those... um. horses. did you see those horses. i bet... did you get a good look at em.

-they were nice horses alright pete.

-no. no. i mean... i didn't mean the horses. i meant did you look good at the whitemen.

-why.

-to see where they were from. to see... to see if they were carryin anythin that might say where they were from.

bug thought about that for a while. -no. he said.

-i bet any money they were from the other side. not only was they on indi... land... indian land. they were on the wrong side of the border.

-so.

-so. pete said -the mounties'll get em. it's federal. they were on the wrong side of the border so the red coats... um. the mounties the red coats'll go after em.'

bug just looked up at the leaves on the tree. he didn't know much but he knew what happened when indians got shot. everybody knew and so did pete. one drunk indian must've shot another drunk indian. that's how it always ended up. so he just looked up at the leaves on the tree. when pete finally got around to being dead bug would drag him deeper into the woods. leave him there. take a day, maybe two for the animals to chew everything up and spread it out so no one could figure out even if they did find one of the pieces. people said bug wasn't too smart but he wasn't so stupid either that he didn't know that if he got any white people involved they'd blame it all on him. too easy. white people couldn't resist making it that easy.

dead was dead and at least the animals would get something to eat.

-maybe this is an elm tree. bug said to bacon pete.

pete burped. let out a little moan. a little dribble of blood and spit ran out of his mouth and down his cheek.

dripped down onto the grass.

bug went over and sat down by pete.

-they don't look like elm. the leaves. bug said -but maybe
it's elm cuz it ain't oak for sure there ain't no oak round
here and if it ain't maple. could be it's elm.
-you're so stupid. pete shouted at bug.
bug didn't answer. he looked up at the leaves some more.
pete burped again. made a sound like a fish when it
comes out of the water.
-i did too... i di... i did too know about the stars. pete
croaked -and my ole man... my... my ole man knew
things... all kinds of... he knew things and he taught me.
pete tried to cough but ended up making a kind of
gurgling sound. like a sick baby.
bug wondered what the leaves might taste like. some-
times tasting things told you an awful lot about them.
bug wondered a lot about what things might taste like.
bacon pete squeezed his eyes shut. tried hard to breathe.
opened his eyes back up again. a little more calm now.
-don't much matter i guess... pete said -...but. uh... i mean...
i guess. about the ole man. he was... gah... he was a drunk.
you were right about that bug. he was just a drunk mostly.
-just like mine. bug said. pete was dying. not long now.
-my old man was a drunk too pete.
-ye... yeah. bacon pete said -just a... shhh... he didn't
know shit.

pete was starting to make a kind of wet growling sound in his throat. like a coyote or a wolverine or something. he was starting to smell pretty bad too. the stink and the blood was starting to bring flies. bug couldn't see them in the dark but he could hear them buzzing.

pete tried to make his hand hit one of the flies but even his hand wouldn't do what he told it to do. so he just looked up at the stars some more.

bug scooted over and put his arms around pete. shooed the flies away as best he could. the smell was bad and pete was covered in blood and shit but bug held him anyway.

-do you b... um... ahh... hey bug. do you believe in... um... in heaven... bug. pete asked him.

bug looked at the tree some more. thought about Pete's question real hard for a while.

-i guess. bug said. -i don't know for sure. but guess i do.

pete started twitching. making all kinds of noises. his eyes rolled back in his head and something black and gooey came oozing out of the hole in his stomach. it smelled kind of like swamp mud. pete was getting real close. his face was white and pale and swollen looking. and his breath smelled awful.

bug just held him.

bacon pete was going to die real soon.

-it's okay pete. bug told him. -don't worry. it's okay.

-no. pete moaned. -i ain't going to... to...

bacon pete let out a long shiver. tried to spit something up. what came out was black and thick like pudding. it just barely made it out of his mouth and then dribbled down his chin. smelled even worse than the belly mud and the mess in pete's pants put together.

bug held bacon pete. he knew what not being able to put your thoughts in the same place felt like and he knew about hurting but this was worse than anything. he just kept holding on to pete and shooing the flies away.

-no. no... pete said -i got... me... i didn't... ummm... i didn't... sh... it... in my... um... pants... i never... nnnn...

-no pete. bug told him -you're right. you never did. i was wrong. you know how stupid i am pete. i know you didn't crap your pants at all.

bacon pete stopped talking and just stared up at the sky. bug wondered why the flies didn't go away. with all the talking and all the noise. the stink. he wouldn't hang around if he was a fly. he looked up at the tree some more and thought about heaven for a while. he always thought dead people just ran around on the earth only you couldn't see them. they were in the woods hunting and running around but you just couldn't see them.

a separate place sounded like punishment to him. why would anybody want to get stuck in one spot where they couldn't leave or run around when they wanted to?

-they sure had nice horses though. bug told bacon pete. they stayed like that for a real long time. looking up at the stars. sometimes at the tree. not a cloud in the sky and after all that rain the stars still seemed like a surprise. every once in a while pete would start talking or try to start talking but more and more he didn't talk. the noises didn't come out of him as much either. but the smell kept getting worse. bug's legs and arms went numb but he didn't mind. he sat holding pete. waiting and thinking about heaven and trees.

the first dawn came. the lying dawn before the real dawn. for a while bug could see the flies. they were everywhere. then the light went away and it was dark again.

in the dark pete said -oh.. hhhhh... hey bug.

-yeah pete. bug said.

-i... um... i. i... i... di... i... didn't mmmmean... pete said -you... yyyyy... um... ain't so... you ain't so... um. i... uh...

-it's okay pete.

they were quiet then. in the darkness. just the flies and the smells and the tree.

finally, the sun started to come up for real. it took it's time though. for a while everything was grey. then it went brown. and then orange. then morning was everywhere. everything was filled with light and bug's eyes hurt from the bright of it all.

bacon pete did a little jerk with his body. coughed. let out a loud burp that smelled worse than anything bug had ever smelled in his entire life.

and then bacon pete stopped breathing.

that was all.

he just stopped.

he made it to morning though.

bacon pete always had to be right.

bug held on to him for a while. watched the world coming back to life.

it was going to be a nice day. the birds were singing and the heat from the sun was already starting to dry things up. you could smell the sunshine. even with all the stink you could still smell the sunshine. the flies even got quiet for a while. bug sat under the tree with his friend and enjoyed the morning.

then he got up to drag bacon pete into the woods.

he stood for a while letting the blood come back to his legs and arms. the flies buzzed around him. he barely noticed them anymore.

bug looked up at the tree for a little.

in the morning light the tree looked different.

not better. just different.

bug stood there staring up at the tree, letting the feeling
come back into his body.

he still couldn't figure out what kind of tree it was.

but bacon pete sure was right about one thing.

it was an ugly tree.

it was about the ugliest tree that bug ever saw.

COYOTE TOOK MY SHOE

coyote took my shoe.
nikakwaho'ta'ː'ah took my shoe.
she wanted my shoe and i gave it to her and now she
went and run off with my shoe.
it's gonna be hard walking back. a long way. and the
railroad track is all pebbles and rocks.
sharp rocks.
hot metal.
that's gonna be hard on my socking foot.
railroad tracks are the best place to find nikakwaho'ta'ː'ah.
she and i been meeting up here for over a month now.
sometimes i give her some of my protein bar. sometimes
we play. sometimes she just wants me to scratch behind
her ears.
this is the first time she wanted my shoe.
this is the first time she took my shoe.
walking back is really gonna hurt.
maybe i should just take the sock off and go bare foot.
maybe i should take the other shoe off and then both
socks but it's all pebbles and stones and the sun has made
the rails too hot and the wood planks between the rails
are probably going to be full of slivers.

i'm going to look mighty silly walking all that way with just one shoe.

i can still see her in the distance with my shoe hanging from one side of her mouth.

that coyote is crazy. everybody knows how crazy that nikakwaho'ta':'ah is.

maybe if i just wait here she'll bring my shoe back.

who am i kidding.

who am it trying to kid.

that coyote is never bringing my shoe back. not today anyways. next time i come back she'll have that shoe all chewed up to bits probably.

that nikakwaho'ta':'ah sure is crazy.

but she's got my shoe and i don't.

and now she's gone.

i can't even see her anymore.

guess it's time to walk home. to hobble home.

man it's gonna hurt.

anybody sees me they're gonna think i'm crazy. only a crazy person would walk around with just one shoe.

but coyote sure looked happy when i let her take it.

it's too hot to walk all that way in bare feet. gonna try with with the sock. at least that way I'll end up with one foot that doesn't hurt.

man this is gonna hurt.

might take me forever to get home.
but i'll probably come back tomorrow or the day after
that.
with different shoes.
i probably won't let her take one of those shoes.
i probably won't.
but then again maybe i will.
maybe i'm about as crazy as that coyote.
maybe i'm about as crazy as that nikakwaho'ta':'ah.
man oh manee man is this gonna hurt.
i sure hope nikakwaho'ta':'ah has fun with my shoe.
i sure hope coyote likes playing with my shoe.

THELMA TWO TOES FELL THROUGH THE ICE

thelma two toes fell through the ice crossing pollys gut.
she wasn't drunk
thelma two toes didn't drink anymore.
the ice crossing pollys gut off island road was usually
solid enough to walk on that time of year. the ice breakers
never came that way and it was just a short walk across
to massena point.
and thelma wasn't getting fat.
the ice just broke and thelma fell through.
thelma two toes almost drowned right away. her nose
and mouth filled up with icy cold water. she sank down
deep in the icy water and couldn't find the hole she fell
through. she dragged herself underneath the ice breathing
the air between the water and the bottom of the ice for
what seemed like forever. a lifetime. luckily she was
wearing a good parka. her legs went all numb and she
lost her mittens so her hands went all numb too.
it was cold that day.
it was real cold that day.

she should have been at the restaurant sweating in the kitchen but on cold days like this hardly anyone came out so myrna could handle the one or two people who did show up. buckshot would show up. that asshole always showed up for his big breakfast and his pie that day was blueberry pie.

thelma had fallen through the ice once before. when she was little. her and myrna were crossing from the island to the city and thelma fell through. back then their mom always made them carry a hockey stick in both hands so thelma didn't fall all the way through. the hockey stick kept her from going all the way. she got frost bite in one foot but they didn't have to cut off any of her toes. their grandpa had fallen through and got frost bite and lost three of his toes on one foot. the priest at the residential school wrote his last name as two toes because that's what everybody on the island called him.

thelma two toes would be lucky if she didn't lose some toes or some fingers.

thelma two toes would be lucky if she got out of this one alive. she knew all the stories about people who fell through the ice and drowned because they couldn't find the hole they fell through. that's why her mother made them carry a hockey stick when they walked across the ice. that's why everybody was always warning about falling through the ice.

thelma toe toes wished she had a hockey stick now.
some kind of stick.
thelma two toes wished she never stopped carrying that hockey stick or some kind of stick to keep her from falling all the way through the ice.
nobody even knew she was out here at pollys gut on the ice.
not even myrna knew thelma was out here.
it would probably take till spring or even summer before her body floated up and got found by somebody. bodies washed up every year that fell through the ice but thelma always thought they had to be drunk to fall through the ice like that. she always figured you got to know the ice and the places you could cross like pollys gut by the time you grew up. if you lived long enough to grow up. you had to be drunk or stupid to fall through the ice once you grew up.
but here thelma two toes was underneath the ice and she wasn't drunk. she felt pretty stupid but she wasn't drunk.
she dragged herself along the ice breathing that thin layer of air and tried to look for the cracks from where she fell in.

thelma remembered her teacher giving them safety tips about falling through the ice like if you were with another person they could pound on the ice so you could find the hole by following the sound. there wasn't anybody to pound the ice for thelma two toes and there wouldn't be anybody to look for her around pollys gut.

she was screwed.

thelma was almost definitely going to die.

her fingers were burning from touching the ice. her legs were so numb she could barely get them to move.

her grandpa used to tell stories about the river and how it used to be something to be scared of back before the whitemen built the seaway. how it would break canoes on its rapids in places like long sault and how the breath of the cold north ocean could freeze you to death in minutes if you weren't careful. how the ice could break for no good reason and the river would swallow you up without anybody even knowing.

but this was the new whiteman's river.

the seaway.

it was tame. it wasn't anything like the mighty river that it used to be.

but that wasn't going to stop it from killing thelma two toes.

-crap. thelma breathed up into the ice. -jesus god crap. jesus god help me.

she thought she felt a crack above her. it was hard to tell with her fingers so numb and burning.

it definitely looked like a crack.

whether or not it was a crack from the hole she fell through was another thing.

thelma took a breath and tried to decide which direction to follow the crack.

a dead sunfish slapped her in the cheek as it washed by her.

thelma decided to follow the sunfish.

one way was as good as the other.

-jesus god. thelma breathed. -jesus god please please help me.

she couldn't think of the names of any of the old gods to pray to so she hoped jesus was listening.

thelma two toes followed the dead sunfish.

hopefully she had more luck than the fish.

BUG ON THE RUN

bug couldn't remember why he was running.

he couldn't remember when he started running.

people made fun of bug for not being able to remember things. bug didn't get mad at them. it used to hurt when people made fun of him but now it just felt normal.

bug wasn't tired.

he hardly ever got tired.

he liked to run. when he didn't have nothing else to do sometimes bug would just run.

maybe that's why he was running now.

maybe he was running away from something.

maybe he was running toward something.

bug couldn't remember.

he had a hard time remembering things.

people said bug got dropped on his head as a baby. he had a scar on his head and he didn't know what it was from. maybe it was from getting dropped on his head.

maybe it was from getting hit in the head.

bug couldn't remember ever knowing where the scar came from.

sometimes bug got headaches. bad headaches. like someone was dragging a knife around the inside of bug's skull. maybe that was from getting dropped on his head if that's what happened.

all bug knew was the headaches were bad. so bad that they would make bug scream out loud sometimes.

running didn't make the headaches go away.

bug kept on running anyway.

one foot in front of the other. and soon you'll be walking out the door.

the path was good here. not just a scraggly deer path. this path had been walked on by people. run on by people. nice and wide. there was still ups and downs to it. this was the woods after all. only place you find flat is in the city.

bug didn't have much use for flat. he didn't have much use for cities. he liked hills and valleys. he liked things to be a little uneven. kept you on your toes.

flat is civilization.

flat is easy.

flat is lazy.

bug was a lot of things but he wasn't lazy. bug was an fbi. a full blooded indian. he didn't want the world to be flat and easy and he didn't expect the world to be flat and easy.

but he liked this path. he liked that it was a little easier than most deer trails. he could let his brain wander a little while he ran.

bug liked it when his brain could wander.

lots of people made fun of bug because of the way his brain wandered. they thought that made bug stupid. maybe they were right. bug figured if he was as stupid as everybody thought he was he probably wouldn't know he was stupid so maybe they were right but that didn't mean it was very nice to make fun of bug.

that's why bug liked pete.

bacon pete.

lots of people didn't like pete for lots of reasons but bacon pete hardly ever made fun of bug for being stupid and even when he did he would fight anyone else who treated bug like he was stupid. maybe that was just because pete liked to fight with other people. maybe it was just because pete was about as foul tempered as a badger. it didn't matter. bug liked that about bacon pete.

bug kept on running.

back in the old days they called them indian runners. whitemen did. they would get indians to carry messages back from one fort to another sometimes over a hundred miles and they couldn't figure out how the indians could go so fast and run so far.

whitemen like things flat and easy.

whitemen never thought about getting off their horses and running even though the land around here was too rough and hilly and the paths were mostly too narrow for horses or men marching side by side in their boots and with their guns.

an indian could run through here a lot faster than any whitemen could figure.

indians didn't call it indian running. they called it dog running. run for a little. trot for a little. maybe even walk for a little. you could go a long way doing it like a dog or a coyote.

mostly bug just liked to run.

sometimes he just started running and kept on running. during the winter he would run across the ice at pollys gut or some other place and run in the woods on the american side where they went on for miles. it wasn't a fast run or nothing. it was more of a jog especially if the wind was blowing hard which it was a lot coming down the river from the north. from the real north. sometimes bug would just run circles around the island.

some people thought bug was training for something. that he was trying to be the next tom longboat. or that he was doing it for exercise.

bug didn't have any reason for running except that he
liked to run.
so he kept on running.
bug kept on running.
he didn't know why he was running.
that was okay.
bug liked running.
maybe he wasn't so smart but bug knew that much.
so he just kept on running.

THANK YOU FOR HELPING US FRY

buckshot liked pie.

he especially liked the pie at the two toes diner.

he liked the all day big breakfast too. bacon. two sausages. three eggs. two pancakes. a biscuit and jam from a jar.

myrna and the other one, the sister who was mostly always in the kitchen, were bitches. they could learn a lesson or two about customer service but they could cook and they made great pies.

most of the time you didn't know what kind of pie it was going to be until you walked through the door. sometimes you could just smell it from the parking lot. cherry. apple. strawberry. sugar. pecan. peach. and buckshot's personal favourite strawberry rhubarb.

the place was a shithole.

ceiling yellow from all the cigarette smoke. dirty windows that you could barely see through. floor could use about ten good scrubbings.

but they sure knew how to make pie.

and they didn't overcook the bacon.

today was cherry pie which was buckshot's second favourite.

he finished his last bit of pancake. buckshot liked his
pancakes with butter and nothing else. no maple syrup.
no jam or fruit. he liked to taste the pancake. he didn't
know why people wanted to spoil a good pancake.
he finished the last few bites and myrna came over.
asked buckshot if he wanted pie.
of course he wanted pie.
myrna didn't talk much except to her sister. buckshot
liked that much about her. it meant not too many stupid
questions. that suited buckshot just fine. but that was a
stupid question myrna always asked.
not once. not fucking once did buckshot not get pie in all
the years he'd been coming to the two toes diner.
buckshot just nodded his head.
myrna leaned forward to pick up his plates and that
stupid pendant necklace hung there for a moment.
buckshot knew what it said.
he knew what it said by heart.
thank you for helping us fry.
stupid.
he even knew the stupid story behind the stupid necklace.
buckshot never asked because he didn't give a shit but
he heard her tell the story to people who asked about
hundred times or so. both sisters had it and it was

supposed to say thank you for helping us fly because they paid for their nephews' first plane trip way back when about a thousand years ago but they got the spelling wrong and they never got it changed. so now it said thank you for helping us fry.

stupid.

but people seemed to love that stupid story. stupid people.

buckshot didn't give a shit if it was true or not. he just ate his big breakfast and his pie and kept himself to himself. myrna was a moody bitch and she spent half her time shouting at her whatshername sister in the kitchen. sometimes she yelled at customers and sometimes she was as friendly as could be. the sister hardly ever came out of the kitchen but you could see whatshername cooking and smoking non stop through the door to the kitchen. lots of the time she looked like she was talking to herself. crazy bitches.

myrna brought the pie and put it on the table in front of buckshot. she didn't ask if he wanted ice cream with it. buckshot never wanted ice cream with his pie. he didn't understand why anyone would want to spoil a good pie with ice cream. pie was pie and ice cream was ice cream. why people wanted to mix them up was beyond buckshot.

myrna wandered into the kitchen and shouted at her sister whatshername for a while and buckshot ate his pie. he took his time and enjoyed every bite.

buckshot didn't like to rush things.

he liked to take his time and he especially liked to take his time with pie.

myrna stood in the doorway for a while shouting at her sister and the sister whatshername shouted back. sometimes they argued in english. sometimes in french. and sometimes they screamed at each other in mohawk. buckshot only understood the english but he didn't even bother listening to that. they were stupid crazy bitches.

the pie was all that mattered.

the pie and the big all day breakfast.

buckshot's mother tried to teach him mohawk. he didn't see a reason to learn a language nobody except people on the island ever spoke. english was just fine as far as buckshot was concerned. everybody seemed to speak that. lots of french people in the city and lots of people on the island who grew up speaking french but buckshot thought french was a stupid language and most of the french people could understand english just fine even if they pretended they didn't.

screw anyone who didn't speak english.

buckshot just wanted to be left alone to enjoy his pie.

it wasn't strawberry rhubarb.

the place was a shithole.

and myrna and her whatshername sister were crazy and
lousy at service.

but the cherry pie was pretty damn good.

and they didn't overcook the bacon.

HANDS

hands.
yours in mine.
mine in yours.
dirty.
our hands. so dirty.
should always clean the hands.
but clean them in what?
clean them how?
touching.
so close.
so very close.
breathing at the same time.
same rhythm.
just the hands.
touching.
connected.
intertwined.
dirty hand in dirty hand.
bodies.
almost touching but not quite.
heat between us.
not just the summer heat.

fine hairs on our necks reaching for each other.
almost touching but not quite.
we lay there our sun darkened bodies by the river.
no words.
we are beyond words.
we are beyond words.
hand in dirty hand we lay by the river.
not quite touching.
barely breathing.
our dark skin against the rocks.
softly the river whispers to us.
softly the river speaks to us.
the dirty water smell the dead fish smell the seaweed
floating reaching through reaching upwards.
dirty place.
dirty rocks.
dirty hands.
but our hearts.
our hearts are clean.
our spirits are clean.
your hand in mine.
small hand in mine.
makes me better somehow.
makes me clean somehow.
even surrounded by all that stink.

even surrounded by all that filth.
you.
make me clean.
you make my heart.
you make my spirit.
you make me.
clean.
the social workers come and call us filthy.
the white people in the city call us filthy.
even some of those on the rez call us filthy.
but when we are together it doesn't matter.
when we are together we are clean.
of spirit.
of heart.
our skin may be dirty our bellies might be empty but
we are together.
and it is enough.
we might be young and may not understand the world
but we know this.
we are enough for each other.
one day we will grow old and we may grow cynical
and even mean.
so many do.
but we will always have this.
we will forever have each other.

we will forever have this time together.
lying on the rocks by the river hand in hand
and almost touching.
we know what this means.
we may be so young but we know what we mean to
each other.
we know what we are to each other.
we know what we are to each other.
hands.
yours.
mine.
touching.
dirty.
but clean.
so very clean.
hands.

BILLY RINGS THE BELL

the guy hit billy bell again.

it wasn't that the guy hit that hard or that he was all at that fast.

ten years ago. five years ago billy bell would've wiped the floor with this guy. but billy's body didn't work the way it was supposed to work anymore. he couldn't walk right and his hands shook so bad most of the time that he tried to hide it by keeping them in his pockets.

this guy thought he was all that he was all that because his punches were landing and billy was bleeding. with all the scar tissue around billy bell's eyes a strong wind could pretty much make billy bleed. the guy was dancing around with his hands down by his waist like he was muhammad ali or something. he was a bum but billy bell was a punch drunk bum and billy just couldn't get his body to show this guy what it was all about.

still.

billy was patient.

on the street or in the ring or in the cage billy bell won a whole lot of fights because he was patient and he could take a punch. could take two or three to land one.

only now it was seven or eight to land one.

billy just kept shuffling forward and the guy kept dancing and throwing lazy punches and billy kept taking the punches with blood pouring into his eyes and sooner or later the guy was going to come in close and billy bell was going to show him what it was all about. it didn't have to be a punch either. if billy got his hands on the guy billy bell had enough wrestling and a little bit of jitsu. all he had to do was get close to the guy. if he could do that even as a punch drunk cripple billy could take this guy if he could just get in close.

billy was patient.

billy bell knew how to be patient.

maybe that was all he had going for him anymore but billy bell knew how to be patient.

he just kept shuffling forward and waiting for the guy to make just one mistake.

the punches didn't even hurt.

billy bell had been in with guys who could really punch and kick and even they hardly ever really hurt. not when he was getting hit. the next day or the day after that one was when it really hurt unless the other guy knew how to go to the body and not many guys knew how to go to the body.

this guy definitely didn't.

this guy thought he was muhammad ali. this guy was definitely not muhammad ali. this guy was nothing. billy bell would've eaten this guy alive back in the day.

but now billy would have to wait.

and billy knew how to wait.

just keep moving the feet and wait.

the guy was trash talking while he was dancing. but billy wasn't listening. he never did.

fighting was fighting.

talking was something else.

billy didn't have any use for talking.

just move the feet and wait.

just move the feet and wait.

and then there it was.

the guy's feet stopped for just a second and billy unleashed the left hook to the body that he'd been waiting on to freeze the guy up. a straight right to snap the guy's chin up. and a left hook to the head to ring the guy's bell all the way.

muscle memory was a beautiful thing.

billy bell might be a punch drunk bum but his muscles remembered how to do things. it just took a while sometimes to get it going.

the guy's knees buckled and billy hit him with a knee to finish it off. the guy's body flopped on the cement like a dead fish. like wet garbage.

splat.

it felt good.

like it must've felt for billy bell's warrior ancestors.

that's what it was all about.

on the rez or in the ring or in the cage that is what it was all about.

billy bell stood over the guy end let his blood drip all over the guy's crumpled body.

he didn't say anything. he didn't need to say anything.

fighting was fighting and talking was talking.

billy bell was a fighter.

a broken down fighter maybe.

but still a fighter.

and this guy.

this guy was not a fighter.

that's what it was all about.

that's all it was all about.

WHY PEOPLE GOT DISEASE

This is not a Mohawk story.

This is a Cherokee story.

It's a good story though. An important story.

It's about when the first People showed up on Turtle Island.

It's about why we have disease and sickness.

How when those first People showed up they got on the other animals' nerves. How they didn't respect the other animals and didn't respect the earth, so the other animals got together around the sacred fire and decided to do something about it.

We like to think that some People are better than other People but as far as animals are concerned People all have to be taught respect. People have to be taught how to behave. People need something to keep them from crowding the planet and doing nothing but harm.

Back near the beginning of People they hadn't learn to respect the earth or respect their animal cousins so all the other animals got together and decided to do something about it.

They gathered in a circle around the sacred fire like I said and passed the talking stick around.

First Turtle took the stick and said – Ho. My brothers and sisters. My cousins and uncles and aunties. I have been carrying you all on my back for a very long time now and you have always treated me with respect. But these new things, these Human Beings, they do not respect their Elders and they do not respect those who were there before them. They throw garbage on my back and they foul the air and they act like spoiled children. I have been very patient for a very long time but these Human beings have greatly tested my patience.

Then Bear took the stick and said – Ho Turtle. I have heard what you said and I know what you say is true. These Human Beings hunt me because they fear me and they do not know that is necessary and right to fear some things, to be in awe of some things. Because they fear me they seek to remove me from Turtle Island. Once I could walk the earth in peace. But now I can find no peace at all since these Human Beings have come.

Then Eagle took the stick and said – Ho my brothers and sisters and all my cousins. You all know me and know that I fly high above and see many things. Once upon a time I could fish in peace and fly in peace but since these Human Beings have come I look down and see them making such a mess of Turtle Island that the fish are all dying and the air is filled with filth and even the sky has broken apart and is sick with their smog and dirt. Next Coyote took the stick and said – I have always been very fond of trouble. You all know this. I like to make trouble and break things and push them over. That is why I helped make People. I thought it would be very funny to have them running around thinking that they were more important than anything else but now I see that they are making all of Turtle Island sick and that they are making so much trouble that I can't even run free and howl at the sky without them hunting me because they are afraid of my tricks. I am very sorry now that I helped make them. I have never been sorry about anything. But now I am very sorry that I did this.

Then Crow took the stick and said – Haw. I like to make trouble as much as Coyote. And I helped make these Human Beings too. But they are more trouble than even I would want. We need to do something to keep these Human Beings from becoming too many and we need to teach them a lesson. We need to teach them to respect life and understand how precious a thing that it is. And I know exactly how we can do that. I will create the first disease. I will make them sick and show them what it is to cling to life and to lose the things that matter most. Haw. That may not be as funny as most of the things I like but even I have had enough of the trouble that they are making.

The stick was passed around the circle and all the other animals agreed that Crow's idea was a good one.

The stick came to Turtle again and she said – Ho Crow. That is a very good idea. I will also create disease and show them what it is to get sick and die. Then maybe they will understand why they should not make the rest of us sick. Then maybe they will learn to respect the life that they have been given. Then perhaps they will respect the Elders as the rest of us do.

Each of the animals took the talking stick and one by one, each and every one agreed that they would each make diseases so that Human Beings would learn to respect and value Turtle Island and everything on it, over it and around it. There would be so many diseases and so many sicknesses that Human Beings could not avoid or stop all of them. Though they might go a time without disease there would always be one that would come along and remind them that life is fragile and precious and without respect and fear and awe it is too easy to forget the thing that are most important.

And when they were done, when every single animal had held the stick and invented a new disease they bowed before the sacred fire and smudged themselves with the sacred smoke and it was done.

And that is the story of how disease came to Human Beings.

It is not a Mohawk story.
It's a Cherokee story.
It's a good story.
It's an important story.

BACON PETE

bacon pete sits up on the old rock on top of big stink hill and argues with the sky.

-what the fuck? bacon pete asks the emptiness -what exactly what fuckin exactly was i supposed to say? huh? in that situation? in that particular fuckin situation?

the sky just stares back at pete. not a real big talker, the sky.

-there I am. bacon pete goes on -there I am and that shit comes down comes down like wham. what exactly did they expect me to do? that's what I'd like to know.

bacon pete gets up off the rock and walks around a bit. stops. sits back down. looks back up at the sky.

-am I wrong? he asks the passing cloud -is that what it is? is there something wrong with me? with the way I'm lookin at this? the cloud just kept on passing.

pete looks down at the houses below. quiet now. not much moving around cept for some skinny old dogs searching through the garbage dump.

-i could be a whole lotta things. bacon pete says to the quiet -i coulda ended up a whole lotta bad ways. been a drunk or a junkie jumpin off the new bridge and splittin

myself in two just outta boredom. gulpin down unleaded
to get high od'in fuckin doin myself

off cuz i'm too stupid to be alive. i coulda fucked up big
time in so many ways but no i hang on to what i'm s'posed
to be what i'm s'posed to do and that ain't good enough?
the quiet don't say nothin. it never does.

-fuck that. fuck them. pete says -i been the only responsible
one around here and you're gonna tell me i gotta step up?
i ain't never fuckin stepped down. fuck you.

bacon pete gets up again. walks up some of that nervous
energy. kicks the old rock with his scarred up worn out
boot.

-i got a job. he hollers at the rock -i got a job how many
people round here got jobs? huh? real ones not fuckin
collectin pop bottles waitin on the welfare check to show
up whinin how the white man's got me down. a real job.
real hard workin paycheck fuckin job. i'm

pretty much the only fucker on the entire rez got a fuckin
real job and i'm getting told i gotta step up? i ain't never
stepped fuckin fuckin down. fuck that fuck you all of youse
i ain't never once stepped fuckin down. fuck that fuck all
of youse.

bacon pete kicks the rock again. he stands there for a while
just thinking. scratches his head. looks up at the sky. at the
cloud already far away. down at the rock. at the old rock.
at the houses.

-fuck. pete says -i know what i gotta do. i know exactly
what i gotta do.
an old bent back dog yips in the garbage dump. not so
much at pete as just at the world in general. the dog yips
again and the limps off behind a pile of garbage bags.
quiet again.
-you think I don't know what i gotta do but I do. pete
says -i do know. i just... fuck.
pete goes quiet. nothing much left to say. said his piece
to the sky and the cloud and the rock and the quiet.
he looks down at the rock. at where he kicked it.
-sorry. pete says to the old rock -sorry rock. i just. the...
just. sorry.
bacon pete stands still for a while. then he takes a big
ragged breath and starts walking back down the hill.
it's still pretty quiet down there.
for now.
yeah.
it's quiet for now.

BLIND

The moon's face was covered with blood and the shadows were long.

I tried to tell them but they could only hear with their white man's ears and they could only see with their white man's eyes.

The word that they use is Civilized.

Civilized means that you can only see in one way and you can only see one world.

Civilized is another word for the white man's kind of blindness.

They could not see the darkness that lurked in the long shadows and they could not feel the rage of the bloody moon.

We were in the land of the Wyandot. The long shadows were filled with the dreams and fears and pain of the Wyandot. The long shadows were filled with Wyandot spirits and the white men could not see or hear or feel the things that belonged to the Wyandot.

My people, the Kanien'keha:ka live close to the Wyandot and, while they have been our enemies for as long as even the oldest stories tell, we have taught ourselves to see with Wyandot eyes and hear with Wyandot ears just as the Wyandot have taught themselves to see with

Kanien'keha:ka eyes and hear with Kanien'keha:ka ears. My people are part of the Haudenosaunee confederacy, the League of Five, perhaps soon to be Six, Nations. We have had government and laws and a way of life but the white men do not consider us Civilized because we do not see the one thing their eyes see and believe in the one thing that they believe.

We are not Civilized because we are not blind.

I tried to warn them.

They wouldn't listen.

White men rarely listen. They are often too busy talking to listen.

When I spoke of the spirits in the long shadows, the spirits in the trees, they laughed and said that was just Indian superstition. They believe a man who was the son of a god came back to life but our beliefs are superstitions. They pray to a dead man on a wooden cross but those who do not are superstitious and Uncivilized.

I have never wanted to be their kind of Civilized. I never want to be that single minded and that blind.

I will not fall on my knees and pray to a dead man hanging from a cross who failed in his mission. Two of their books say that he cried out "My God! My God! Why hast thou forsaken me?" Among my people being tortured is a test of your strength and their son of a god failed that test. "My God! My God! Why hast thou forsaken me?" He wailed. Our children are stronger than their greatest man. Our women would scorn and laugh at their saviour. I would not worship such a man. Such a son of a god. He broke and he cried out. He let the enemy see him break. That is an unforgivable sin among my people. Even among the Wyandot. Most of them have fallen to their knees for the black robes who cannot not see the spirits in the shadows and in the trees.

But the Wyandot are still not blind and Civilized. Not yet.

They are worthy of respect and honour.

Many Wyandot have fallen to their knees for the blind white man way of seeing the world, but many still have not.

I have not. I could still see the darkness in the darkness and the blood on the moon. And I could hear the spirits and I could feel the spirits.

They are foolish people.

And I tried to warn these white men, who at least do not wear the black robes.

They wouldn't listen.

None of them would listen.

They think that their thunder sticks make them invulnerable to what they could see and even what they could not see. But their sticks will not make thunder in the rain. That is funny to me. A stick that can only make thunder when it's not raining. And it was raining.

It had been raining for more than a day.

It is still raining.

Even if they were working their thunder sticks would probably be no more use against the things that come out of the darkness than our knives and clubs and arrows. The spirits of the darkness are not subject to the ways and weapons of our world and they cannot be killed or wounded like those who lived in this world, the only world that the white men can see.

The white men dismissed the spirits because they hadn't thought of them. They dismissed the Windigo because they hadn't thought of it. They dismissed the Skinwalker because they had not thought of it.

That's what it is to call yourself Civilized.

I stepped to one side of the trail and let some of them pass. They looked at me with laughter in their eyes and they would not listen. I was not going to be the first that the spirits of the darkness took.

I have proved my courage in battle. I have proved my courage against men.

You cannot fight spirits when you are surrounded by those who cannot see them and so I let the Civilized white men pass from the darkness to the deeper darkness.

It is a simple thing to die.

It is no simple thing to have your spirit taken from you. I stood back and let the white men walk into the darkness that was darker than the shadows.

I have fought in many battles. I have faced death at other men's hands again and again. I am no coward. But spirits do not care if you are brave or strong or if you are a coward. Or if you are Civilized. They will take you just the same. I do not know if a white soul is the same. Perhaps it is different and the spirits do not hunger for it. Perhaps a white soul is undercooked. The colour of their skin, like the underbelly of a frog, does seem soft and undercooked.

I do not know about such things.

I know what it is to measure and respect a man even as you are killing him or torturing him. I know this because I have lived it and because my ancestors have lived it and it is in my blood. I do not think respect is in these white men's blood. I do not think that it is in their bones. They show no respect for their enemies and they show no respect for the spirit world. They do not even show respect for each other.

No man can really know a spirit. Not even his own.

We are all blind in that way, but these white men, these Civilized men seem so much more blind than others.

The darkness within the darkness and the deep silence are the only sign that spirits linger and it is a thing to chill the blood. That is a thing to make even the bravest man or woman pause and let others pass him by.

The white men walk forward as if they cannot see.

I hear the first scream and my spine begins to tremble.

I hear the second scream joined again by the first and I know that I was wise to be afraid.

The night grows darker and the screams rise and linger and echo in the terrible silence that follows and fills the night.

The rain continues to fall.

And I am afraid.

I am frozen to the place that I stand.

I can smell the blood and urine and feces and too a smell that I have never known and hope to never know again.

It is far more foul than the other smells and it makes me gag.

I do not know if it is the fear that I smell or the spirits themselves. I have never heard tell of such a smell.

The morning is very far away.

The moon is bloody and the shadows are long and dark and rain beats down unforgivingly.

My skin is damp. Not just from the rain. My legs are weak. My stomach lurches towards my throat and my bowels quiver and I do not move.

I know that if I move I will die or something will happen to me far worse than dying.

I can make out pieces of torn and bloody flesh in the darkness.

I will stand here until the morning comes or until the spirits come to take me. I will stand here as long as I can stand and I will not move.

I tried to warn them.

I tried to tell them.

Now it is too late for them to listen.

Now it is too late for them to see.

Only the night can hear me now and I will make no sound.

Only the night is listening and something else.

Something that lurks in the darkest part of the darkness.

It waits.

It lurks.

And I wait.

I tried to warn them.

I tried to make them see.

They were blind and they were Civilized.

And now there is nothing left but the darkness.

The lurking silence.

That I cannot see and cannot hear.

I too am blind.

I am alone.

And all that there is for me...

Is the night.

And the darkness that is darker than the night.

And the waiting.

The endless waiting.

SLUSHIE

slushie was worried about the blood.

it was a nice carpet and he didn't want to ruin it by getting his blood all over it.

he would have got up and gone outside to bleed but he couldn't stand up.

if his auntie was home he'd apologize but she was probably at the casino so he had no one to say sorry to.

he couldn't remember exactly how he got to his auntie's house but he could remember there was some kind of fight. a knife or something sharp. he could remember that one of the bell brothers was there. and that his auntie's house was the closest place he could drag himself to. he hoped she wouldn't be too mad at him if he died before she got home. she was always particular about her rugs and slushie was worried he was ruining her rug and she would be angry about that or maybe angry that he even came to her place to die.

there was a lot of blood.

a lot of slushie's blood.

it would be a shame to ruin his auntie's carpet.

slushie was always a bleeder. a lot of his fights back when he was fighting got stopped early because of the blood. that never seemed right. some guys bleed easy and some guys don't. nothing to do with what kind of fighters they were.

his face was all scar tissue now. cauliflower ear. one foot dragged because of the brain damage. people on the rez made fun of the way slushie looked which was why he got in most of his fights now.

he couldn't remember if that's how this fight got started.

he couldn't get up.

he couldn't remember falling down or why he fell down. sometimes he fell down for no good reason.

doctor told him one day he was going to fall down and never get back up again if he didn't stop fighting. one good punch was gonna shut his brain down for good.

the world was spinning around slushie.

the world was almost always spinning for slushie.

his brain was broken.

slushie was broken.

and he was bleeding all over his auntie's carpet.

he hoped he didn't die here. his auntie would be really mad if he died on her floor. she was already gonna be mad about the blood.

slushie tried to get up. tried to lift his head. tried to sit up. ended up rolling onto his side and then on his back. felt like puking. didn't want to choke on his puke like a rock star. didn't want to puke on auntie's carpet.

he couldn't remember who he got in the fight with.

one of the bell brothers maybe.

whoever it was gave him a beating. cut him too. cut slushie up good.

once upon a time beating slushie up wouldn't be so easy. nowadays almost anybody could beat up on slushie. hell, nowadays slushie could fall down all on his own. cracked his head open a few times just falling down on his own.

he was twitching all over.

could be a seizure coming. felt like it could be a big one. maybe the one to end it all.

that wouldn't be so bad if he wasn't in his auntie's house. why the hell did he come here. what made him come to auntie's house to bleed all over and maybe die.

he could smell something burning. he could taste burnt copper in his mouth. could definitely be a big one. a real big one.

slushie was okay with dying. he'd been okay with dying practically since the day he was born. so much pain. all his life so much pain. being dead had to be better than slushie's life.

he just didn't want to die on his auntie's floor.

she was a good woman. the only person that ever treated slushie half decent. she didn't deserve all that blood and a dead body on her floor.

what kind of asshole goes to his aunties to bleed all over the place and die.

slushie tried to get up.

he couldn't remember if he tried to get up before or how many times he tried to get up but he tried anyway. maybe with a bit of luck, if he tried really hard. maybe he could make it to his feet and out the door and then to the woods or someplace and auntie would never know who had bled all over her carpet.

slushie told his muscles to move. he ordered them to move. but they didn't. in fact he was pretty sure nothing on his body moved even a little bit. he couldn't remember how he got here or why he came here but it seemed like a pretty good bet he was going to die here.

auntie was going to be so mad.

that woman had a temper on her.

she didn't even drink which was a good thing because as mean as she got sometimes she'd probably get a lot meaner if she was a drunk.

mostly she was a good woman.

mostly she was kinder to slushie than anyone else had ever been. she took him in when he had nowhere else to go and when he was little and he needed to hide from the old man she would take him in and give him a safe place to sleep.

which was why slushie was so sorry that he was bleeding all over his auntie's carpet and that he was going to die on her floor.

she'd be mad for sure but she was about the only one that was going to care one way or the other that slushie was dead. slushie was real sorry to be such a burden to her. he should of gone to the woods to die or some hill or the river or someplace like that. not here to his auntie's house.

he was cut open bad.

he couldn't remember who it was that cut him open. maybe that bell brother. they were mean like that and they sure liked knives and sharp objects. one of the bell brothers had cut off all but three of his own fingers playing around with knives. he couldn't remember which one. another one had cut off his own big toe with an axe playing some kind of stupid axe game. those bell brothers liked their knives and their axes and they were all about as mean as could be.

maybe it was the bell brother.

slushie couldn't remember.

somehow he had made it to his auntie's place for some reason he didn't even know why.

mostly she was a real good woman.

slushie didn't know why he would do this to her.

auntie was real particular about her house too. kept it clean as a whistle.

and now here slushie was bleeding all over her carpet and she would never be able to get all that blood out.

slushie thought he might of shit himself too. but that was inside his clothes.

still.

the stink would be pretty bad.

hopefully she wasn't gone somewhere for a long time. sometimes she went up north to work the casino up there. slushie hoped she wasn't gone up north. his body was going to stink up pretty fast in this heat. he might bloat up and ooze stuff all over the place.

and the flies.

one time slushie's cousin ugly bobby died and they
didn't find him for almost two weeks. there was flies
everywhere and the stink was so bad it made people
puke themselves and stuff had oozed out from ugly
bobby's body all over the floor. even though it was a tile
floor and not a carpet they couldn't get the stains out
between the tiles.

slushie tried to get up again.

he couldn't remember if he tried before or what happened
if he did try or when the last time he tried if he did try.

no deal.

nothing moved.

nothing at all.

so slushie just lied there.

bleeding on his auntie's carpet.

it was probably going to be ruined.

the carpet.

slushie was sorry about that.

he was real sorry about that.

his auntie would be mad at first.

she would forgive him and miss him.

she would be the only one that missed him.

slushie was real sorry about that too.

but mostly he was sorry he was getting blood all over
his auntie's carpet.

slushie was mostly sorry about that.

INDIAN DONUTS AND TEA

There was a knock knock knocking at my door.

You might even say a tap tap tapping.

I should've known better than to answer that door.

I knew I knew even before I opened it that it would be Nikakwaho'tà:'a, Coyote and Tsó:ka'we, Crow.

When those two get together there's nothing but trouble coming. You should run and hide if Crow or Coyote, if Tsó:ka'we or Nikakwaho'tà:'a, show up at your door. You should shoot yourself in the head if they both show up at the same time.

I'm just kidding. Don't shoot yourself.

But definitely run and hide.

Definitely run and hide.

Either one of those two is trouble at your door. But when those two crazy tricksters get together...

Oh, manee... man, man.

It's nothing but bad news.

And it was Nó:ya, New Year's Day.

Well I thought it was Nó:ya day.

You kind of lose time in Tsothohrhkó:wa, in January, in the Big Cold. Things run together, time runs together and gets confused when you get trapped inside by all that cold and snow.

So I thought it was Nó:ya for some reason. I was sure it was New Years Day or something like that.

New Year's Day on the Rez is like Hallowe'en. First people to show up at your door you have to give them Kahsherhón:ni, Indian Donuts, and Tea. That Coyote and that Crow were definitely after donuts and tea. And those two crazies eat everything you put in front of them and what they don't eat they steal so you better have lots of donuts.

I didn't have so many donuts.

I hardly had any donuts.

I knew that was going to be trouble for sure.

Nikakwaho'tà:'a and Tsó:ka'we just walked right in.

They just walked right in.

–You got any Kahsherhón:ni for us? –Coyote asked –Any Nó:ya donuts for us? I'm hungry for Nó:ya donuts real bad.

-Haw haw haw –Crow said –Of course he has Kahsherhón:ni for us. He must have Nó:ya donuts. And some tea. Sweet tea for us. Haw.

-If you don't have Kahsherhón:ni for us, maybe you got some Tim Hortons donuts. I would eat some Tim Horton donuts even though they're not as good as Kahsherhón:ni. I like them Timbits a lot.

–Nikakwaho'tà:'a said –They don't dip so good in tea but they're mighty tasty.

I didn't have Tim Hortons donuts.

–Nó:ya donuts. Nó:ya donuts. –Tsó:ka'we said. –Haw haw haw. Everybody knows they have to be Nó:ya donuts so we can dip them in the sweet tea.

I had enough Kahsherhón:ni for me, for one or two people. Those two, Coyote and Crow, could eat enough for twenty. Maybe a hundred. And it was too late to run and hide. Those two would find me right away and there would be plenty trouble to pay.

There was going to be plenty trouble anyway.

–Boy oh Chef Boyardee Boy. – Coyote said –I can taste those Indian Donuts now.

–Haw haw haw. –Crow said –I like the ones shaped like people. I like the ones shaped like Bears and Wolfsand Turtles. I can pretend I'm eating people and Bears and Wolfs and Turtles and it makes me happy. Haw haw haw. I can't wait for them Nó:ya donuts.

Tsó:ka'we and Nikakwaho'tà:'a started dancing around celebrating the donuts they were going to have and the sweet tea.

And then it occurred to me.

And then I remembered.

I had been making Kahsherhón:ni even though it wasn't New Year day. Nó:ya was the day before. Or the day before that. Maybe lots of days before that. I was confused because I was making the donuts but only because I wanted some and making the donuts had made me think it was Nó:ya day too.

Those two, Coyote and Crow, probably showed up because they smelled the Kahsherhón:ni and that made them think it must be New Year's day. Things got pretty confusing in the winter. Cooped up inside against the cold. Everybody is on Indian time in Tsiothorkó:wa, in January.

–Hey. –I said –Heya guys. Crow. Coyote too. It's not Nó:ya anymore. You showed up too late. you must be on Indian time. I do have some donuts but not many. And I can sure make you some sweet tea but it's not New Year's day. That already passed.

–Haw. Haw haw haw. –Tsó:ka'we said –You people. You human beings are so silly in your thinking. Every single day is Nó:ya day if you make it Nó:ya day. Especially in Tsiothorkó:wa.

–Yeah. Yeah yeah. –Nikakwaho'tà:'a said –You just bring out those donuts and sweet tea and let us worry about what day it is. And if we run out of donuts you can go to the Tim Horton's and get us some of those whitemen donuts. Those are pretty good too. Not as good as Indian Donuts but pretty darn good some of them.

It was cold out. It was snowing. I didn't want to try to drive to Tim Horton's for donuts.

Crow and Coyote started doing their dance again. Around and around the room. –Yay. –they sang –Yippee and Yay and Haw haw haw. It's donut time. It's donut time! And the best time in the world is donut time!

That crazy Tsó:ka'we and Nikakwaho'tà:'a danced and sang for a long time. Maybe hours. They knocked over all the furniture and broke my TV and they just kept on dancing and singing. They jumped up the tables and chairs and broke those too and they just kept on dancing. Singing. Breaking everything and dancing and singing. Let me tell you, you don't ever want to let Coyote and Crow into your house and you definitely don't want to let them into your house together.

And then, when everything was smashed and broken, they stopped.

–All that dancing. –Nikakwaho'tà:'a said –All that dancing and singing sure worked up my appetite.

–Haw. –said Tsó:ka'we – How come you don't have the donuts out for us? And the sweet tea. What kind of host are you that you don't even have the donuts and sweet tea ready for us when we finish singing and dancing.

Haw? We did singing and dancing for you and you don't even offer us donuts and tea?

I went into the kitchen. I knew better than to argue with those two. I made some sweet tea and brought the donuts and they gobbled them up in minutes. Maybe seconds. All those donuts I was going to have for myself were gone and my place was a mess.

And now they probably expected me to go to Tim Horton's to get them more donuts. Out there in the cold and my car probably wouldn't even start.

–Haw. –Crow said –Those were pretty good donuts. Those were definitely pretty good Indian donuts.

–Boy oh Chef Boyardee Boy. –Coyote said –I sure did like them donuts. And that sweet tea.

I put on my coat and my big boots. Grabbed my car keys.

–Don't forget the Timbits. –Nikakwaho'tà:'a said –I really like those Timbits.

–Haw. –Tsó:ka'we said –And while you're gone we'll do some more dancing and singing.

And they started dancing and singing right away.

I opened the door.

The cold outside hit me in the face.

Let me tell you.

Let me warn you.

If you hear a knock knock knocking on your door one
night in Tsothohrhkó:wa, in January.
Maybe even a tap tap tapping.
Don't open the door.
Run away and hide.
Because unless you have more Kahsherhón:ni, more
Indian Donuts than you know what to do with and all
the sweet tea in the world.
Even then.
Even then.
Run away.
Take my advice and run away and hide.
And don't.
Whatever you do.
Don't answer that door.
If you hear a knock knock knocking.
Or a tap tap tapping.
In Tsiothorkó:wa.
In January.
Maybe anytime.
Run and hide.

Also by Jules Delorme

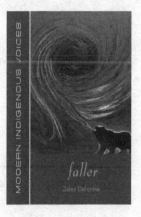

9781772311747 - paperback
5.5"x 8.5" | 120 pages
$19.95
POETRY
9781772311754 - ePub